WOMEN IN AVIATION

Julian Hale

SHIRE PUBLICATIONS

Bloomsbury Publishing Plc

PO Box 883, Oxford, OX1 9PL, UK

1385 Broadway, 5th Floor, New York, NY 10018, USA

E-mail: shire@bloomsbury.com

www.shirebooks.co.uk

SHIRE is a trademark of Osprey Publishing Ltd

First published in Great Britain in 2019

A catalogue record for this book is available from the British Library.

ISBN: PB 978 1 78442 363 6
          eBook 978 1 78442 364 3
          ePDF 978 1 78442 361 2
          XML 978 1 78442 362 9

19 20 21 22 23   10 9 8 7 6 5 4 3 2 1

Typeset by PDQ Digital Media Solutions, Bungay, UK

Printed and bound in India by Replika Press Private Ltd.

Shire Publications supports the Woodland Trust, the UK's leading woodland conservation charity.

COVER IMAGE

A woman pilot of the Air Transport Auxiliary (ATA), *c*.1943. (Fox Photos/Hulton Archive/Getty Images). Back cover: Tracey Curtis-Taylor flying *Spirit of Artemis* over Herne Bay at the Amy Johnson Memorial Airshow in 2015. (Smudge 9000/CC BY-SA 2.0)

TITLE PAGE IMAGE

A pre-war image of Pauline Gower and her colleague Dorothy Spicer inspecting *Jason III*, the Gipsy Moth in which Johnson attempted to fly to Siberia shortly after her Australian adventure.

CONTENTS PAGE IMAGE

Apart from Jacqueline Auriol, Barbara Harmer is the only woman to have flown Concorde and the only one to do so on a scheduled airline service.

ACKNOWLEDGEMENTS

All pictures are courtesy of Getty Images, except for those on pages 4, 6, 7, 8 (both), 18, 23, 24 (right) and 27, which are Public Domain/Library of Congress; and the two images on page 61, which are Public Domain/NASA.

CONTENTS

INTRODUCTION

THE STORY OF women in aviation goes back further than many imagine. Women flew aboard hot-air balloons in the eighteenth and nineteenth centuries and were involved in powered flight from the beginning: Katharine Wright is sometimes referred to as 'the third Wright brother'. In later years, Amelia Earhart, Amy Johnson and others flew all kinds of aircraft, in all weathers and in all parts of the world, proving that they could fly just as well as their male counterparts.

Their struggle was not easy. Although the women pilots of the British Air Transport Auxiliary received support from most quarters (and sometimes incredulity instead of resentment), others did not. Members of the American Women's Airforce Service Pilots – WASPs – encountered hostility in many forms from male servicemen, including the reported sabotage of aircraft. Yet attitudes evolved steadily: by the 1970s, women were flying as airline captains, air force pilots (in the USAF) and even undergoing astronaut training.

This book is intended as a primer on the subject. The whole story of women in aviation would necessitate a much larger volume and would include the often-overlooked contributions made by women from all countries and in all fields of aviation – design, manufacture, testing and support – not just flying. Nevertheless, it is to be hoped that this book will introduce the reader to some of the famous (and a few of the lesser-known) personalities who have done so much for women and aviation in the past.

OPPOSITE
Katharine Wright, 'the third Wright Brother', with her brother Orville in an aircraft in 1915. Although largely forgotten, Katharine played a significant role in the Wrights' success.

THE EARLY YEARS

On 16 April 1912, a woman dressed from head to foot in a purple satin flying suit, climbed into an aircraft at Dover, took off and promptly disappeared into a thick cloud. Fifty-nine minutes later, her aircraft touched down in the Pas-de-Calais. Her name was Harriet Quimby and she had become the first woman to fly an aeroplane across the English Channel.

Quimby had shown great resolve – several aviators, including the famous Gustav Hamel, had attempted to dissuade her from making the perilous crossing (he even offered to make the flight himself, dressed in Quimby's trademark suit). Yet her achievement was overshadowed by

Harriet Quimby became the first woman to fly the English Channel in an aeroplane in April 1912. Her flight unfortunately, in terms of publicity, coincided with the *Titanic* disaster.

the sinking of the *Titanic* on 15 April and Quimby never received the publicity she deserved. Only three months later she was dead, when her two-seat Bleriot monoplane inexplicably pitched forward during an air display in the United States, throwing Quimby and her passenger to their deaths. She was thirty-seven years old.

The story of women in aviation stretches back to the eighteenth century. Frenchwoman Elisabeth Thible became the first woman to fly in an untethered hot-air balloon in Lyon in 1784. Sophie, wife of the famous pioneer balloonist Jean-Pierre Blanchard, became famous for her lighter-than-air exploits, but died while unwisely giving a firework display from her hydrogen-filled balloon over Paris in 1819.

The first woman to be awarded a pilot's licence (in 1910) was also French: Elise Raymonde Deroche, often styled pseudonymously as Baroness de Laroche. Her career, which was notable for her survival of three near-fatal accidents, ended in tragedy when she crashed to her death in 1919.

In 1911, Hilda Hewlett became the first British woman to qualify as a pilot. She was born Hilda Herbert in 1864, married Maurice Hewlett in 1888 and developed an interest in motor cars. The couple met Gustav Blondeau at a motor meeting in 1909 and befriended him. The pair attended Britain's first aviation meeting in Blackpool in October 1909 and, inspired, sought instruction in France before returning to the UK. They established the Hewlett & Blondeau flying school at Brooklands, among

Harriet Quimby in her trademark purple satin flying suit. Only months after her Channel crossing, she was killed in a flying accident in the United States.

RIGHT
Sophie Blanchard
was the most
famous of the
early female
balloonists.
Her signature
performance
was a firework
display from her
hydrogen-filled
balloon, the last
of which ended
tragically in 1819.

FAR RIGHT
Elise Raymonde
Deroche became
the first woman
to gain a pilot's
licence. Her
career was
dogged by a
series of flying
accidents.

whose famous pupils was Thomas Sopwith. Hewlett won several flying competitions and in a maternal first, taught her own son to fly. It is also said that there were no accidents at her school at Brooklands – a remarkable achievement.

Hewlett and Blondeau also started their own aircraft manufacturing business before the First World War and the firm grew to become a major licenced manufacturer

BESSIE COLEMAN

In 1921, Bessie Coleman became the first African-American woman to earn a pilot's licence. After moving to Chicago, she wanted, in her own words, to 'amount to something' and chose flying. Racial prejudice forced her to take flying lessons in France, where she successfully completed a ten-month course three months early. For the next five years she toured the USA, barnstorming and speaking at many churches and schools about race and aviation. She fought continually against racism, refusing to appear at air displays where the crowd was segregated. Tragically, while on a test flight on 30 April 1926, the mechanic flying her aircraft lost control and she fell from the cockpit to her death. Her legacy lived on with the establishment in 1929 of the Bessie Coleman Aero Club in Los Angeles, where among others, members of the famous 'Tuskegee Airmen' learned to fly.

of other companies' aircraft. It was at this point that she 'politely separated' from her husband (who had earlier said that 'women will never be as successful in aviation as men. They have not the right kind of nerve.'). She became known locally for driving a large car with her Great Dane in the back seat, dressing 'eccentrically' and cropping her hair 'short in a masculine style'. The factory made a great contribution to the British effort during the First World War, employing some 700 staff and producing over 800 aircraft. However, in common with many aircraft companies, the firm was unable to survive the post-war slump and Hewlett & Blondeau closed in 1920.

Hewlett emigrated with her family to New Zealand in the 1920s, where she established an airfield and flying club in Tauranga. In 1932, she flew as the first female passenger between New Zealand and the UK (the journey, via Jakarta courtesy of KLM Royal Dutch Airlines, took eleven days). The first great British female aviation pioneer died in 1943 and as requested, was buried at sea.

An official ban was placed on civilian flying at the beginning of the First World War. But pioneers, such as Harriet Quimby and Hilda Hewlett, had shown that women could, against the expectations of some, fly as well as their male counterparts. Nor did they lack 'nerve', in an era when flying was at its most hazardous. Nevertheless, it was in the aeroplane's 'Golden Age' following the First World War that women would truly earn their place in aviation history.

Although she died aged just thirty-four, Bessie Coleman's legacy lived on with a flying club named in her honour.

THE FLYING LADIES

In May 1928, a small Avro Avian biplane landed at Croydon Aerodrome. From it stepped a tall figure with an odd assortment of luggage. She was Mary, Lady Heath, and she had just become the first woman to fly from Cape Town, South Africa, to London.

The First World War had provoked a surge in aviation development and the potential of the aeroplane was obvious. Many new aviation routes were pioneered by record-setting flights during the 1920s. The bravest went alone: in May 1927, Charles Lindbergh became the first to fly solo across the Atlantic, setting a trend for similar attempts over the next decade.

In 1925, the formidable Lady Heath (at the time Mrs Eliott-Lynn) became the first woman to receive flying lessons at the London Aeroplane Club at Stag Lane in north London. There, Eliott-Lynn befriended another female aviator. Lady Bailey, whose husband was the South African millionaire Sir Abe Bailey, was some ten years older than Mrs Eliott-Lynn and a mother of five. She was 'charming, vague and dreamy' and was already approaching middle age when she learned to fly. Both she and Eliott-Lynn collaborated to establish an altitude record for light aircraft, flying the first of the latter's Avro Avians.

Following her divorce and first husband's death, Eliott-Lynn married Sir James Heath and the couple sailed to South Africa, taking her Avian with them. She enthusiastically

OPPOSITE
Lady Heath was a staunch advocate both of women and the value of commercial aviation. It was her friend Lady Bailey, however, who was decorated for her services to aviation.

Lady Heath with Lady Bailey after setting a joint altitude record for light aircraft in 1927. Their achievements may have been similar but their characters could not have been more different.

promoted aviation in Africa – at the Johannesburg Aero Club, where there was a flying meeting in her honour, the crowd became so excited that it trampled down the barriers and invaded the airfield.

On 17 February 1928, Lady Heath's Avian took off from Pretoria for the UK. The little aircraft was heavily loaded with equipment and luggage, including: spare parts for the engine; a medical kit; a collection of novels; a Bible; a shotgun with fifty rounds of ammunition; six day dresses; silk stockings; a hat and fur coat; and a pair of tennis rackets (although it is unclear what use these would be on the journey).

Near Bulawayo, in present-day Zimbabwe, she suffered sunstroke, landed the Avian without remembering doing so and regained consciousness underneath a thorn bush to find three local women dabbing her forehead with milk. She was then escorted across Sudan by a male pilot, Lieutenant

Lady Heath photographed immediately after landing at Croydon at the end of her Cape Town–London adventure. Only later was a bullet hole discovered in one of the Avian's wings.

Bentley, as it was forbidden for women to overfly the country alone. When over Nairobi, she threw her tennis rackets and some novels overboard to lighten her aircraft as it struggled to gain altitude in the hot climate. Later, a temperature of 40°C, combined with turbulence, made her physically sick while

Lady Heath smiles after her successful Cape Town– London flight in 1928. Due to her forthright manner, the former Mrs Eliott-Lynn was known by unkind critics as 'Lady Hell-of-a-Din'.

The 'delightfully vague' Lady Bailey joined the ATA at fifty but although 'quietly brave, deceptively casual [and] defiantly eccentric', she was forced to resign within a week of joining on age grounds.

over the Nile. During the flight to Cairo, she ate chocolates and read a novel, which proved so absorbing that she almost missed the airfield altogether, where a large reception had been prepared for her. On landing, she donned a pair of silk stockings to 'smarten' her appearance before leaving the Avian's cockpit.

She continued her journey along the North African coast. A seaplane escort promised by the Italian *Regia Aeronautica* failed to materialise and so Bentley accompanied her on the leg between Tunis and Naples. Mindful of the possibility of making a forced landing in the Mediterranean, she wore a pair of inflated motorcycle inner tubes around her waist and was fortunate she did not need them, for they were over-inflated and burst at 7,000 feet.

Lady Heath arrived at Croydon on 17 May and 'stepped from her machine looking as fresh as a daisy, wearing a fashionable day dress, the fur coat and a black straw hat' and was quoted as saying, 'It is so safe that a woman can fly across Africa wearing a Parisian frock and keeping her nose powdered all the way.' It was only at Croydon that a bullet hole was discovered in the Avian's fabric – Lady Heath had been shot at, probably over North Africa.

As Lady Heath flew one way, so Lady Bailey flew the other. The two in fact crossed paths at Khartoum before Lady Bailey was escorted across Sudan by Lieutenant Bentley. She later became lost and landed at Tabora (in present-day

Lady Bailey's demeanour was a contrast to that of her friend and rival Lady Heath. Arriving at Cape Town, she apologised for her late arrival 'due to getting muddled up in the mountains.'

Lady Bailey on her arrival at Croydon from South Africa in February 1929.

Tanzania) in the blaze of the midday sun and, misjudging her approach, crashed her de Havilland Moth so heavily that it was beyond repair. Sir Abe sent a new Moth out to her from Cape Town, and a few days later, she set off again. Despite a bout of influenza, she arrived at Cape Town on 30 April. Her first remark to her husband was: 'Hello Abe, how are you?', after which she apologised for her late arrival 'due to getting muddled up in the mountains.'

A few months later, without any fanfare, she flew back to Croydon, after a journey in which she was 'agreeably surprised at finding a string of aerodromes as far as Dakar.' Perhaps this lends credence to Amy Johnson's comment that:

She never appears to organise a flight or even to have any clear idea where she is going…she is the most delightfully vague, will-o'-the-wisp Ladybird, but she always gets there somehow, even if she has to go to the length of waiting for an entire new machine and engine to be sent out to her when her own has crashed.

Of Lady Bailey and Lady Heath, it was the latter who, through her tireless advocacy of aviation and women, did most to advance their cause. In 1927, *Flight* magazine wrote that: 'It is still a common prejudice for women as aviators to be rather disdained. Mrs Eliott-Lynn has perhaps done more for her sex in [the] squashing of this prejudice than any other woman.' Yet, Wendy Boase argues that 'Lady Heath… never lost an opportunity to win publicity. She had a worthy cause…but her self-advertisement made her unpopular with the press and public.' By contrast, Lady Bailey's 'modesty only served to create wilder excesses of enthusiasm' and it was Bailey who was made a Dame of the British Empire for her services to aviation.

Amelia Earhart (centre) in London after her solo transatlantic flight in 1932. Lady Bailey stands on the far left while Dorothy Spicer and Pauline Gower are on the right.

'LADY LINDY': AMELIA EARHART

MEANWHILE, THE UNITED States was captivated by the achievement of Charles Lindbergh and within a year another attempt, with a woman on board, was planned. A publisher called George Putnam stepped in and, according to his own version of events, proposed a young woman of his acquaintance. Her name was Amelia Earhart.

Back in December 1920, Earhart had accompanied her father to a flying meeting in California, and the next day, she took her first flight in an aircraft. She later wrote, 'As soon as we left the ground I knew I myself had to fly', and she quickly booked flying lessons at a nearby airfield. In April 1928 Earhart went to an office in Boston, where she was asked if she would like to be the first woman to fly the Atlantic.

Despite her protests that she should be allowed to take the controls for at least part of the flight, Earhart was to be a passenger while Wilmer Stultz and Louis Gordon were to crew *Friendship*, their Fokker trimotor seaplane. Earhart's own possessions for the flight were minimal and included a toothbrush and comb, two handkerchiefs and a small bag of oranges. She took a camera and Putnam lent a pair of binoculars. Most importantly, she borrowed a heavy fur-lined flying suit, which was several sizes too large but protected her from the cold inside the Fokker's cabin.

Unfortunately, the weather was so poor that the Fokker was unable to take off from Trepassey Harbour, Newfoundland, until 17 June. Earhart, earplugs in place, spent most of the

OPPOSITE
'Lady Lindy'.
Amelia Earhart became a major celebrity during her career and she continues to inspire generations of women and aviators to this day.

Wearing her borrowed flying suit, Earhart stands with Wilmer Stultz and Louis Gordon after their transatlantic crossing in 1928. The other two were soon forgotten as Earhart was elevated to celebrity status.

flight in the empty main cabin, squeezed between two large fuel tanks, for conditions were reportedly too treacherous for her to take the controls. As dawn came, the liner SS *America* was spotted a few miles away and the *Friendship* circled, while Earhart scribbled a note asking for their position, tied it to one of the oranges and threw it at the ship. It missed, as did a subsequent attempt. The crew discussed the possibility of landing alongside the *America* but with the sea so rough, they knew that the Fokker would never get airborne again and so they flew on. Ironically, *America*'s captain had just ordered that their position be painted in large white letters on the deck, but before this could be done the aircraft turned away.

After a further anxious hour and a half, the shadow of land emerged from the mist. Finally, their fuel almost exhausted, the weary crew spotted a large bay and landed. Almost an hour later, the first boats came out to the aircraft, and to the crew's surprise, revealed that they were not in Ireland but Burry Port, South Wales. It was here that the press began to gather and where the moniker 'Lady Lindy', coined by Putnam, was applied to Earhart. In the first of many similar incidents, an unseen hand reached out as Earhart walked through the throng and to her surprise pulled the silk scarf from her head.

Putnam had syndicated the story and it appeared on the front page of newspapers around the world. Earhart remained modest and despite her protestations that 'I was a passenger on the journey – just a passenger', the two men were soon forgotten as Earhart was pulled into a dizzying round of engagements. Among the many telegrams and letters was one from Lady Heath: 'Dear Miss Earhart…if you phone me I'll throw down whatever I'm doing to come and fly with you or talk…Ring me!' Shortly afterwards, Earhart secretly tested Heath's Avian at Croydon and was so impressed that she purchased it for $3,200.

On their return to New York, the *Friendship*'s crew were given a ticker-tape parade. Now, Earhart would never again be able to 'go about freely, unrecognised.' Yet despite the adulation, there were some in the press who were determined to discount the achievement. George Putnam, who married Earhart in 1931, devised a plan to answer her critics: a solo flight across the Atlantic.

Although Earhart's decision to make a solo Atlantic crossing may have been to prove herself the best female pilot of her day, there was strident opposition to the plan, notably from Lady Heath, who wrote a magazine article entitled 'Why I Believe Women Pilots Can't Fly the Atlantic'. However, by the time the article reached the newsstands, Earhart had already taken off at the controls of a Lockheed Vega, exactly five years to the day after Lindbergh's own departure from New York. Among the few possessions she took with her was an elephant toe bracelet, given to her by Putnam in 1929, which she regarded as a good luck charm.

A few hours after leaving Newfoundland, the Vega's altimeter failed; Earhart now had no true indication of her height – a vital factor in instrument flying. A severe storm buffeted the Lockheed, then the exhaust manifold began to vibrate due to a faulty weld. Earhart looked under the cowling and saw flames fluttering in the darkness. She later wrote that she was 'sorry she had looked at the break at all because the flames appeared so much worse than they did in the daytime.' The vibration worsened during the night, which added to her concern. At one point she considered turning back.

Well-wishers surround Earhart in Ireland following her solo Atlantic crossing in 1932. After altimeter failure, serious icing and a broken fuel line, Earhart was glad to make landfall.

Earhart stands on the deck of the French liner *Ile de France* during her return from Europe in 1932 with her husband, the publisher and publicity guru George Putnam.

Earhart flew on, sipping at a small can of tomato juice and using smelling salts to keep her awake. She later entered cloud and climbed to fly above it. Slush formed on the windscreen as the aircraft began to ice up – a highly dangerous phenomenon – and the Lockheed quickly entered a spin: 'How long we spun I do not know,' wrote Earhart. 'I…regained flying control as the warmth of the lower altitude melted the ice. As we righted and held level again, through the blackness below I could see the whitecaps, too close for comfort.' Two hours from her estimated landfall, she turned on the reserve fuel tank, to find the fuel gauge leaking, pouring a steady drip of petrol on to her shoulder. The vibration from the damaged manifold increased, and mindful of the possibility of a fire

from the flames, she decided to land
at the first available opportunity.
Earhart made landfall over County
Donegal, in north-west Ireland, and,
avoiding a number of grazing cows,
landed in a field. As she climbed
out of the Vega, she spotted a farm
labourer approaching. 'Where am
I?' she called. 'In Gallegher's pasture'
came the geographically exact reply.

Earhart was required to don her
flying coat again the next day and
taxi the Vega around the field, before
stopping once more and emerging, for
the benefit of the newsreel cameras.
Another tickertape procession awaited
her in New York, followed by the award
of the Distinguished Flying Cross.

Earhart and
New York
Mayor Jimmy
Walker during
the enthusiastic
celebrations
which greeted
her on her
return to the
United States
after her solo
Atlantic flight.

By 1934, her Atlantic flight was 'old news' and she began
to plan a new and daring flight. One evening, according to
Putnam, she looked up and said, 'I want to fly the Pacific
soon.' 'You mean from San Francisco to Honolulu?' Putnam
asked. 'No,' she said, 'the other way, it's easier to hit a continent
than an island.' 'When do you want to do it?' he replied.

Putnam engaged the experienced Hollywood stunt pilot,
Paul Mantz, to oversee the technical preparations. When
news eventually broke of her intention, considerable negative
publicity resulted, with many seeing the flight as nothing
more than a self-serving exploit. Ten pilots had already lost
their lives attempting to make the same crossing; to improve
Earhart's chances, Mantz installed a two-way voice radio
aboard the Vega.

On 11 January 1935, Earhart took off from Hawaii. The
flight, in contrast to her Atlantic crossing, was uneventful and
she was delighted with the new radio. Her welcome was as

NATIONAL
GEOGRAPHIC
...TY

ABOVE RIGHT Earhart with the Mollisons and the Roosevelts, in a photograph taken during their visit to the President's retreat at Hyde Park.

ABOVE LEFT Earhart and Eleanor Roosevelt. Both were staunch advocates of women in aviation, and Mrs Roosevelt later took a special interest in the WASP during the Second World War.

rapturous as ever; among her letters of congratulation was one from President Roosevelt, which read: 'You…have shown even the "doubting Thomases" that aviation is a science which cannot be limited to men only.'

Earhart and Putnam now had a round-the-world flight in mind, although when a reporter expressed the hope in 1935 that she would not make any further trans-oceanic flights, she replied, 'Why? Do you think my luck might run out? Do you think luck only lasts so long and then lets a person down?' After corresponding with a variety of aircraft companies she chose the new, twin-engined Lockheed Electra 10E, a modern aircraft for its time, with an enclosed flight deck, retractable undercarriage and all-metal construction. However, it was expensive and sponsorship was sought from a number of companies. At no stage was the flight sponsored by the US Government, either for scientific purposes or, as some have since suggested, for more nefarious reasons.

The Electra was fitted with the most sophisticated radio and navigation aids of the day, including a two-way radio. Nevertheless, the aircraft was described as 'a physically taxing aircraft to fly' and Mantz, who spent many hours with Earhart,

'was never entirely satisfied with her ability to fly the Electra...
despite his personal respect for her.'

Earhart and the experienced veteran maritime navigator
Harry Manning planned to fly west from California. However,
the distances of the Pacific posed a problem and a southern
route was planned, flying from Hawaii south-westwards to
New Guinea via the tiny, virtually uninhabited Howland
Island. The route would then be relatively straightforward:
to Australia, through south-east Asia, across India, along the
Persian Gulf, over Africa to Dakar and then to South America,
leaving an easy final leg to California.

It was possibly Mantz who suggested that Fred Noonan,
an ex-Pan-Am Clipper navigator, with much experience of
the South Pacific, should accompany them until the Electra
reached Howland. It has since been alleged that Noonan
left Pan-Am as a result of his heavy drinking; this is untrue.
Although stories of his heavy drinking circulated, Noonan was
in fact a first-class navigator.

Earhart flew without incident from California to Hawaii
on 17 March 1937. However, on take-off the following day,

Amelia Earhart
standing in front
of the Electra in
which she went
missing. Her
disappearance,
with navigator
Fred Noonan,
continues to fuel
speculation to
this day.

the Electra ground-looped and the undercarriage collapsed. The damaged aircraft was recovered and the three returned to the United States.

After consideration, the flight plan of the second attempt was reversed and Earhart was to fly east due to weather conditions in the Caribbean and Africa. By this point, the costs 'were frightening', and Earhart wrote that 'friends helped generously…[but] I more or less mortgaged my future. Without regret however, for what are futures for?'

On 21 May 1937, Earhart departed again, somewhat hurriedly, for a planned arrival back in the USA on 4 July. Mantz was not consulted and many last-minute details were skipped, including the throttle settings for each leg of the flight, which were essential for governing fuel consumption. There were also concerns over Earhart's knowledge of the Electra's radio – Manning knew how to operate the system

Earhart and Paul Mantz in 1937. Mantz later wrote of his misgivings about her flight, citing concern over a lack of adequate preparation.

Earhart's Lockheed takes off from Oakland, California, for the first leg of the world flight to Hawaii. This initial attempt ended days later when the Electra was damaged on take-off.

but it was Noonan who flew with Earhart during the second flight. An instructor recalled that an attempt to formally instruct Earhart was curtailed by another appointment and 'We never covered actual operation such as taking a bearing with a direction finder, not even contacting another radio station.'

The cramped nature of the Electra's cockpit, in combination with constant engine noise, hours of concentration and lack of sleep, left Earhart exhausted during the round-the-world flight.

Earhart stopped at Miami for a week before departing again. While there, she confided to a young reporter that: 'I have a feeling that there is just about one more good flight left in my System and I hope this trip is it. Anyway, when I have finished this job, I mean to give up long-distance "stunt" flying.'

The early stages of the flight proceeded smoothly and they left Natal, Brazil, to fly to Dakar on Senegal's west coast. As the Electra neared Dakar, Noonan, working in the cabin behind the cockpit, passed a note to Earhart advising her to turn south. However, her instinct placed them too far south and when they reached the African coast, she turned north. Within 50 miles, she realised that she had made a mistake and landed at St Louis in Senegal. If Noonan's instruction had been followed, they would have arrived at Dakar only a little later than scheduled. Although Earhart admitted her error, her reliance on instinct rather than on Noonan's calculations did not bode well.

Nevertheless, the flight across Africa was uneventful and the pair proceeded to Aseb, Eritrea, on the west coast of the Red Sea, before the long flight to Karachi. As it was

Earhart and Noonan stand with a map showing the ill-fated Pacific leg of their flight. Contrary to myth, Noonan was a 'first-class navigator' and Earhart wrote of his 'uncanny powers' of navigation.

forbidden for Earhart to land on Arab territory, she carried a specially written note in case of a forced landing, which disingenuously stated that she was on an important mission for His Majesty King George VI and that on no account must she be harmed.

From Karachi, the pair negotiated difficult monsoon conditions, before arriving at Bandung in modern-day Indonesia where, during a further delay due to bad weather, some of the Electra's instruments were repaired, including the flowmeter. This had apparently 'given trouble previously, on several occasions…' but would be critical on the long legs across the Pacific.

On 27 June, Earhart left Bandung for Darwin, Australia, where the Electra's direction finder was serviced. Two days later, they reached Lae, New Guinea. There, the groundcrew for Guinea Airways, who had experience servicing Lockheed aircraft, gave the Electra a 'thorough going over'. Earhart noted that 'everyone has been as helpful and co-operative as possible – food, hot baths, mechanical service, radio and weather reports, advice from veteran pilots…'

On 30 June, Earhart and Noonan repacked the aircraft, leaving everything considered unessential to the upcoming flight, even down to her lucky charm, the elephant toe bracelet Putnam had given her years earlier. Survival equipment, including the flare pistol and ammunition, was also unloaded. In a telegram sent that day, Earhart referred to 'Radio misunderstanding and personnel unfitness', a sentence which has frequently given rise to speculation about Noonan's condition and the possible effect of alcohol, but it could have referred to Earhart's own condition after 22,000 exhausting miles with a further 7,000 miles remaining.

Earhart calculated that the 2,556-mile journey from Lae to Howland would take around 18.5 hours; they aimed to arrive no later than 7.30am at Howland. Both Noonan and Earhart recognised the challenge of the upcoming flight and she wrote that 'Howland is such a small spot in the Pacific that every aid to locating it must be available.' To assist Noonan's navigation, the USS *Ontario* was located between Lae and Howland and the USCGC *Itasca* was stationed off Howland Island itself. A new direction finder was in place on Howland Island and manned in expectation of guiding the Electra as it drew nearer. Unfortunately, it was in use throughout the night and by daybreak had run out of power.

At 00.00 hours Greenwich Mean Time (GMT was used to simplify the problem of flying across different time zones: it was 10.00am in Lae and 12.30pm on Howland) a visibly exhausted Earhart took off from Lae. The aircraft was probably loaded with 1,000 gallons of fuel, giving some twenty to twenty-one hours of flying time. Another pilot waiting to land at Lae saw the heavily laden Electra lumber down the runway and cross a dirt road near the end of the take-off run, the camber of which caused it to bounce up before dropping over the sea, where it flew so low he reported the propellers were 'throwing spray'. Nevertheless, another witness reported that 'it was obvious the aircraft was well-handled and pilots of Guinea Airways who have flown Lockheed aircraft were loud in their praise of the take-off with such an overload.' Others remembered that the dust kicked up by the Electra over the runway did not disperse immediately but hung in the hot, still air for some time.

There were strong headwinds that day and although the Electra would have been capable of maintaining 150mph over the last 1,700 miles or so (as the fuel load decreased), the arrival time at Howland would have changed to approximately 20.38, leaving little margin for error.

Earhart gave a position report at 07.20 GMT, which placed her near the Nukumanu Islands and on track for Howland; this was the only positive position from Earhart during the entire flight. After this, there is no absolute certainty concerning the track of Earhart's Electra, giving rise to many outrageous theories over her disappearance.

As agreed, *Itasca* received a number of voice messages from Earhart at half-hourly intervals. Although the *Itasca* sent messages back, Earhart did not acknowledge them and she was on air too briefly for radio bearings of her position to be taken. Moreover, if she did not receive the messages, and she did not appear to do so, she would have been unable to take any radio bearings of her own. At 18.15, Earhart reported that she was 'About 100 miles out.' The *Itasca* expected the Electra to appear some time around 19.30 but nothing was heard from her until 19.12 when, at maximum signal strength, she reported: 'We must be on you but cannot see you but gas is running low. Been unable to reach you by radio. We are flying at altitude 1,000 feet.'

At 19.28, Earhart radioed: 'We are circling but cannot hear you…' This time the response from *Itasca* was acknowledged by Earhart, but she was apparently unable to obtain a radio bearing. She then requested *Itasca* to take a bearing on the Electra but it was unable to do so. *Itasca* began making heavy black smoke, which stretched at one point for 15 miles and was easily visible, to provide Earhart and Noonan with a visual reference. Subsequent messages from the *Itasca* went unacknowledged.

At 20.14 Earhart's voice was heard for the last time. She spoke rapidly and some listeners described her transmission as sounding 'hurried and almost incoherent.' She said: 'KHAQQ to *Itasca*. We are on the line of position one five seven dash three three seven. Will repeat this message on 6,210 kilocycles. We are running north and south.'

What happened after this remains a mystery. *Itasca* made continual efforts to make contact until 21.30, when it was decided that Earhart must have ditched and the search procedure was set in motion.

Earhart and Noonan may have flown within visual range of Howland but possibly could not see it for cloud or strong sunlight. The Electra probably ditched within 100 miles of the island and most believe neither Earhart nor Noonan survived. At the personal authorisation of President Roosevelt, a massive search was launched, involving nine naval ships and 66 aircraft, which lasted several weeks. George Putnam gained authorisation for more searches to be made, but as the months went by, even he began to lose hope. Dozens of islands were searched in the months after Earhart's disappearance but all were uniformly unsuccessful. Putnam eventually resigned himself to accepting that his wife had died.

Amelia Earhart's last flight, her disappearance with Fred Noonan and their ultimate fate continue to fuel speculation to this day.

In 1997, on the centenary of Earhart's birth and sixty years after her disappearance, Linda Finch paid tribute by successfully flying a Lockheed Electra around the world.

AMY, WONDERFUL AMY

ONE OF AMELIA Earhart's friends, in a letter home in July 1937, wrote: 'No more flights, so no need to worry! Poor Amelia!' The writer was Amy Johnson, Britain's own 'Queen of the Air'; the words disguise her shock at the loss of her 'friend and mentor'.

Amy Johnson was brought up in comfortable respectability in the town of Hull. By 1927, seeking new horizons, Johnson left for London, where she took a job as a typist at a large law firm. A few months later, while on a bus to the Hendon air display in north London, she alighted at the Stag Lane Aerodrome. Immediately bitten by the 'flying bug', she joined the London Aero Club and began to learn to fly. One of her instructors was James Baker (of Martin-Baker fame) and fellow pilots at Stag Lane included ladies Heath and Bailey. As well as flying and navigation, Johnson was fascinated by the technical side. She spent many hours in the hangars and she eventually earned the licences necessary to allow her to maintain and inspect a number of different aero engines. On 9 June 1929, she went solo for the first time.

Her world was severely shaken, however, by the suicide of her sister Irene the following month and she seemed to begin planning a solo flight to Australia at this time.

Through Sir Sefton Brancker (Director of Civil Aviation at the Air Ministry), Johnson was able to secure backing from a number of sponsors, most notably from Charles Cheers Wakefield (Lord Wakefield) of Castrol. The chance visit of

OPPOSITE
Johnson poses with *The Desert Cloud*, the elegant de Havilland Puss Moth in which she eventually broke the London–Cape Town record previously held by her husband, Jim Mollison.

Amy Johnson worked hard to obtain qualifications allowing her to inspect and maintain aircraft engines. She works on one here, probably at Stag Lane, north London, before her Australian journey.

Johnson stands in front of *Jason* before her flight to Australia. She always referred to *Jason* in the first person and 'he' was painted bottle green to match her flying suit.

a journalist to Stag Lane on 8 January 1930 turned Johnson into a minor celebrity, when she told him of her intention to fly to Australia.

Johnson continued with her preparations, including the purchase of a bottle green flying suit from Lillywhite's on Piccadilly Circus. On 23 April, she paid for a de Havilland Gipsy Moth, registered G-AAAH, which she christened *Jason* (after her father's business telegraphic address) and repainted bottle green, to match her new suit. Extra fuel tanks had been fitted by the previous owner, giving *Jason* an endurance of thirteen hours. Johnson made countless notes for her journey, only to find later that many were hopelessly out of date. In addition, she packed a mosquito net; a tropical flying helmet;

extra boots; tinted goggles; inner tubes; a cooking stove; billy cans; flints; a revolver and ammunition; a first-aid kit; and an air cushion.

On 5 May 1930, the heavily laden biplane took off from the grass runway at Croydon – Johnson's target was the UK–Australia record of 15.5 days set by Bert Hinkler in 1928. The *Daily Mail* reported excitedly but inaccurately that she was 'taking off with a cupboard full of frocks', that she was 'golden-haired' and informed its readers that she was twenty-two, taking four years off her age. Meanwhile, it doubled the flight's distance to 22,000 miles.

Johnson aimed to beat Hinkler's record by flying straight across Europe to Turkey, then to India via Iraq. Her first stop was Vienna where, intimidated by the mechanics at the airfield, she was prevented from overhauling *Jason*'s engine herself. Refuelling *Jason* was a lengthy task, using a succession of petrol drums, with the petrol being poured through a filter and strained through two chamois leathers. The fuel often overflowed through the air vent, soaking her luggage.

From Istanbul, where she was kept waiting for 1.5 hours while her papers were endlessly checked, Johnson flew south-east to Syria and, while flying over the Taurus Mountains, she suffered one of the greatest shocks of her journey.

Entering thick cloud, she climbed to find clearer skies, only for the engine to splutter, forcing her to fly lower. Shortly afterwards, she found herself in a narrow ravine, her compass spinning wildly. *Jason* entered more cloud and emerged with one wing down and on

A friend, possibly Jack Humphreys, helps to fasten Johnson's parachute before she left Croydon at the start of her epic solo Australia flight.

course for a sheer rock face. Johnson swerved just in time and although she soon emerged into brilliant Syrian sunshine, the experience left her shaken.

Johnson later force-landed somewhere between Aleppo and Baghdad, when she lost sight of the River Euphrates in a sandstorm. With utmost difficulty, she positioned *Jason* into the wind, tied the little biplane down and covered the engine. Later, she heard barking, and mindful of tales of travellers being torn apart by stray packs of dogs, she cradled her revolver as the sand raged around her. Eventually, the storm cleared but, in her haste to take off again, she dropped several of her precious tools, which were immediately swallowed up by the drifting sand. She finally landed hours later at Baghdad, where an undercarriage strut snapped on landing. This was repaired overnight, but the following day, it broke again when she landed at Bandar Abbas. Johnson, by now struggling with exhaustion, supervised the filling of *Jason's* oil tank, as she had every night since the journey began five days earlier. It was hours before any of the necessary Castrol XXL could be found and 2.30am when she went to bed; she rose again at 4.00am for the next leg to Karachi, where she would begin her journey across India. Her time to Karachi set a new record, beating Hinkler's record for that stage by two days.

From there she aimed to fly to Allahabad in one day but she landed several hundred miles short, at Jhansi. With daylight fading, she quickly took off again but realised she had insufficient fuel for the journey. Reluctantly she turned back but, unable to find the airfield, was forced to make a last-moment landing on an army parade ground. According to eyewitnesses, her out-of-control aircraft touched down, whereupon it charged some soldiers and careered towards their barracks, narrowly missing a telegraph pole and scattering more men preparing to mount guard. A wing tore through a noticeboard before the little aeroplane eventually jammed itself between two barrack buildings. Fortunately, a carpenter was able to repair the wing and motor cars brought fuel from the airfield ten miles away.

Two days later, with fuel and daylight again running out and unable to find her landing ground on the racecourse at Rangoon, Johnson attempted to land on a football field. *Jason* careered into a ditch, breaking the propeller, an undercarriage strut and, most seriously, badly damaging a lower wing. She was lucky, however, as students from the nearby Government Technical Institute were able to repair the wing and undercarriage while a replacement propeller was fitted. *Jason* was then laboriously moved 12 miles to the racecourse.

Johnson flew onto an airfield near Bangkok, but on her next leg to Singapore, poor weather and strong headwinds forced her to land at Singora, some 400 miles short of her destination. The time lost meant that she no longer had a chance of beating Hinkler's record. From Singapore, she intended to fly 1,000 miles to Surabaya but became lost and frightened over the Java Sea:

> I seemed hemmed in by blackness…unable to go on, equally unable to turn back or stay still, I circled round and round. I was more than terrified and shrieked aloud for help. I didn't want to die that way – I knew that thousands of hungry sharks were waiting…my fingers closed over the knife I had in my pocket.

Fortunately, the sun broke through the clouds and Johnson was able to reorient herself, landing at a sugar plantation some 200 miles west of Jakarta. A KLM airlines Fokker guided her to Surabaya in Java, where a faulty magneto forced her to stay for two nights. On her penultimate leg she became lost again, causing anxiety among those who were expecting to receive her in Atamboea in Timor. In fact, she had landed among giant anthills, outside a remote village 12 miles from Atamboea. There followed another daunting take-off from an

Jason lands at Port Darwin at the end of Johnson's gruelling solo flight. At this moment, she became a celebrity – aviation would drive her on for the rest of her life.

improvised airstrip to the airfield, before she could prepare for the final stage of her journey the next day – the 500 miles across the Timor Sea.

Six hours after leaving Timor, *Jason* appeared over Darwin. As she landed, a reporter rushed towards the deafened aviator and asked, 'Well, what shall I tell the dear old world?' Before she could answer, the crowd surged forward, engulfing *Jason* and his tiny, exhausted pilot: like Amelia Earhart two years earlier, never again would Amy Johnson be able to go about unnoticed.

Johnson's achievement caused an outbreak of euphoria around the world, which, in the twenty-first century, is difficult to appreciate. Despite her exhaustion, she was forced to make a tour of the major Australian cities in *Jason*, before she suffered a severe landing accident at Brisbane. After this mishap, she continued her tour as a passenger; one of her pilots was Jim Mollison, who asked her to dance with him at a ball in Sydney. Johnson was deluged with tributes: songs were written about her (including the famous 'Amy, Wonderful Amy'), items of clothing were, briefly, named after her and women imitated her hairstyle. She received gifts and cheques, including one from the *Daily Mail* for £10,000, and even proposals of marriage. In Britain, she was presented with two new aircraft, which she named *Jason II* and *Jason III*.

Although 'the British Girl Lindbergh' had, overnight, become perhaps the world's most famous aviator, she was aware that she was only as good as her last flight. A few months after her Australian adventure, she foolhardily announced she would fly from Britain across Russia to China, in the middle of winter. In the event, she crashed *Jason III* in Poland. She continued by train to Russia, where she was feted as a model for Soviet womanhood. She tried again later in 1931 in *Jason II*, a de Havilland Puss Moth, and flew with a mechanic all the way to Tokyo. This extraordinary accomplishment, which took only 10.5 days, was completely successful. The pair toured Japan before flying back to the UK. However, her triumph was negated by a record-breaking flight from Australia to the UK by another aviator: Jim Mollison.

Johnson met Mollison again while she was holidaying in South Africa, where he had crash-landed at the end of a record-breaking flight from London to Cape Town. Four days after she arrived back in the UK on 4 May 1932, they became engaged, when Mollison proposed to her over lunch at Quaglino's, a fashionable London restaurant. He later wrote:

> In Australia she was the ex-typist who had become a famous pilot – a person whose hair became windblown; whose nails got dirty; and who often smells of petrol… Now, across a red-lighted luncheon of the choice foods and white linen, she smiled back at me, a manicured, powdered, waved blonde.

They were married later the same year.

Amelia Earhart's solo transatlantic flight quashed Johnson's own plans in that direction. Instead, she decided to try to break Jim's London–Cape Town record. At the controls of a new de Havilland Puss Moth, *The Desert Cloud*, she set out in November 1932, flying the faster but considerably more dangerous western route over Africa. Despite her lack of sleep (she flew by moonlight as well as by day), Johnson successfully navigated thousands of miles, including the forbidding Sahara Desert, with only minimal assistance at remote outposts when she landed, to arrive in Cape Town four days and seven hours after leaving Lympne, almost half a day ahead of Mollison's record. Incredibly, she then flew back in just over seven days, surviving on little more than black coffee and caffeine tablets.

The impulse that drove Johnson, as well as others such as Earhart, Beryl Markham and Jean Batten, was a need to avoid becoming 'old' news.

BERYL MARKHAM

Beryl Markham, famous for her love of adventure, as well as her romantic liaisons, was brought up in Kenya, where she learned to ride so well that a local tribe named her 'Lady of the Horses'. After a short-lived marriage, Markham took up flying and in 1936 won renown for flying the Atlantic solo, against the prevailing winds, from east to west. After writing her memoirs she retired into obscurity. In 1983, her book, *West with the Night*, was reprinted to acclaim, allowing Markham to live in comfort, until her death in 1986.

Beryl Markham with her Vega Gull, *The Messenger*, before her Atlantic flight.

It was this need which led the Mollisons to fly together from the UK to New York in July 1933. Although the flight, which began at Pendine Sands on the Welsh coast, began successfully, strong headwinds meant that by the time their aircraft, a de Havilland Dragon named *Seafarer*, was approaching New York, it was down to its last reserves of fuel. Finally, after more than forty hours without real sleep, the exhausted couple attempted to land in semi-darkness at Bridgeport, 40 miles north of their intended destination. After five aborted approaches, Mollison

'England's most famous flying couple.' Amy and Jim photographed before they flew their de Havilland Dragon, *Seafarer*, from Pendine Sands to a crash-landing in New York.

committed to a landing, but as the aircraft touched down they realised, too late, that they were landing with the wind. *Seafarer* tore helplessly across the airfield before crashing into a ditch. Amy was saved by her seatbelt but Jim was thrown through the windscreen as the aircraft turned over. Rescuers found her cradling him in her lap, while she called 'Hurry, please, we're over here…hurry, please.' In fact, although he was knocked unconscious, Jim was not badly injured and Amy was almost unharmed.

Amy and Jim Mollison recover following the crash of *Seafarer* at the end of their Atlantic crossing. Hours after their arrival, the hospital was 'under siege' by reporters.

Amelia Earhart listened to the live radio broadcast from Roosevelt Field. When the announcer revealed that the couple had in fact crashed at Bridgeport, she exclaimed, 'they deserved better luck', before quickly packing some clothing to take to Amy. Although their arrival had been marred by their accident, they still took America

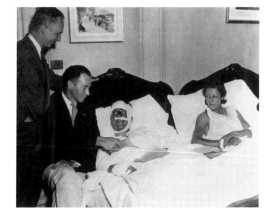

Amy and Amelia Earhart after the Mollisons' Atlantic crossing in 1933. 'They deserved better luck', commented Earhart on hearing of the couple's crash-landing.

Amy and Jim Mollison surrounded by onlookers in front of *Black Magic* before the MacRobertson race in 1934. Failure in the race and Jim's drinking did their marriage further harm.

by storm: a baby born locally that night was christened Amy Mollison Stafford. Their star power was increased by Earhart's arrival at their hospital and the white roses sent by the Roosevelts. The Mollisons later stayed with Earhart and Putnam and both couples were invited to lunch with the Roosevelts at their Hyde Park retreat. Over the following weeks, Earhart and Johnson became close, discussing the former's plans for an airline and attending engagements with the Ninety-Niners, a club formed by the first women to fly in the USA.

But the Atlantic flight which ended in a ditch also signalled the beginning of the end of the Mollison marriage. The pair entered the MacRobertson UK–Australia Air Race in October 1934, in which they shared *Black Magic*, a sleek and fast twin-engined de Havilland Comet. However, after leading the first leg to Baghdad, they were forced out of the race

when unsuitable fuel caused engine problems in India. The Mollisons were furious with each other when *Black Magic* reached Allahabad, and raised voices could be heard from the cockpit as race officials approached the Comet. While Amy broke down in tears, three empty whisky bottles were allegedly found next to Mollison's seat. Over the

following year, Johnson's concerns over her husband's drinking and (suspected) infidelity grew: later that year she returned home early one evening to find him inebriated and sprawled on their bed with another woman.

In 1936, Johnson decided to set another solo UK–Cape Town record to promote her idea for a new airline, Air Cruises, this time at the controls of a Percival Gull, equipped with a radio. She approached the *News of the World* for an exclusive story deal, but record-setting flights no longer garnered the publicity (and money) they once had. Nevertheless, she boarded the Percival wearing a suit designed by Schiaparelli, which she described as combining 'smartness with utility'. The attempt was aborted when the little

The Mollisons with *Black Magic* at Allahabad after their retirement from the MacRobertson race. Their body language hints at the irrevocable differences emerging in their marriage.

In this photograph, Johnson poses (rather uncharacteristically) in one of the outfits designed for her by Schiaparelli before her 1936 flight to Cape Town.

monoplane crashed on take-off at Johnson's first stop, the remote French airfield at Colomb Béchar on the northern edge of the Sahara. She immediately made plans for another attempt and garnered favourable press coverage as a result of her 'press-on' spirit (reminiscent of Jean Batten). The second attempt the next month was successful: she arrived in Cape Town after three days and six hours, beating the previous record by eleven hours.

Jean Batten arrives at Lympne after her solo 1936 New Zealand–UK flight. This was her last record-breaking flight. Her glamorous appearance and reclusive nature earned her the soubriquet 'the Greta Garbo of the skies'.

JEAN BATTEN

A determined and courageous aviatrix who broke hearts as well as records, Jean Batten grew up in New Zealand. Although her first attempt to beat Amy Johnson's UK–Australia record in 1933 ended with a crash in India and a second flight ended in a mishap in Italy, her third attempt (which earned her the nickname 'Try Again Jean') beat Johnson's record by five days. She later beat the UK–South America record, navigating with only a watch and compass, and the UK–New Zealand record too. An intensely private person, she later faded into obscurity and died in 1982.

By the late 1930s, long-distance flying was beginning to lose its appeal to the public and war clouds were clearly gathering, lending the later years of the decade a more sombre aspect. Johnson broke no more records after her Cape flights. Plans for a transatlantic flight (carrying the film of King George VI's coronation to the US) and a world flight both came to nothing. Her divorce from Mollison was finalised in 1938 and she increasingly spent much of her time in France. In May 1939, she began working as a pilot for the Portsmouth, Southsea and Isle of Wight Aviation Company, earning a pound a day plus flying pay; the press pointed out that one could now fly with Amy Johnson for a mere five shillings.

The beginning of the Second World War in September 1939 stopped further civilian flying. No more records would be broken for the foreseeable future. The 'Golden Age' of flight, which had perhaps begun to lose its lustre amid the routine of passenger air travel as well as the uncertain political climate, had come to an end.

Johnson receives acclaim in London, following her record-breaking flight to the Cape and back in 1936. However, public interest in record breaking was beginning to wane.

Johnson with Anna Neagle on the Welsh Harp reservoir in 1931. Interestingly, Neagle would go on to play Johnson in the 1942 film *They Flew Alone* made shortly after Johnson's death.

SPITFIRE GIRLS

T HE MUNICH CRISIS of 1938, at which a European war was only narrowly averted, served as a catalyst for a number of changes in the world of aviation. A director of British Airways (BA), Gerard D'Erlanger, proposed the formation of a reserve of pilots who, due to age, infirmity or gender, would be ineligible to serve but could fly VIPs, mail and medical supplies around the UK, thus freeing RAF pilots for front-line duties. His proposal was enthusiastically adopted. D'Erlanger was made head of a new organisation, the Air Transport Auxiliary (ATA), which operated under the control of the British Overseas Air Corporation (BOAC) and BA. By August 1939, D'Erlanger had the foundations of his organisation in place.

The expected bombing of the UK at the outbreak of war did not materialise and the ATA was rapidly given a different role: that of delivering aircraft, both old and new, to and from factories and squadrons. At the same time, the idea of recruiting women into the ATA was mooted. Although the RAF was initially resistant, a women's branch of the ATA (soon to be nicknamed the 'Always Terrified Airwomen' by some) was formed in November 1939, at first with only eight pilots. A competent and well-connected woman was needed to lead the new section.

Pauline Mary de Peauly Gower was inspired by aviation when only nineteen and, forsaking her role as a debutante, began to take flying lessons, much against her father's wishes.

This famous image was taken by the press in January 1940. One of the women recalled that they were asked to 'scramble' to their Tiger Moths, before repeating it for the photographers.

In 1930, she joined the London Aero Club at Stag Lane and met Amy Johnson, who had recently returned from her UK–Australia flight. She also met Dorothy Spicer, with whom she launched a fare-paying 'joyriding' business. They later set up 'Air Trips', probably the first aviation company owned and staffed by women. Amy Johnson, at a loose end in the late 1930s, considered joining Gower and Spicer's company but dismissed the idea, writing, 'nice girls but little money to be made.'

After her mother's death, Gower gave up the joyriding business, wrote a book on women in aviation (to which Amy Johnson contributed a foreword), served on several committees and became a well-respected authority on aviation. As the country prepared for war in 1939, Gower was chosen to head the women's section of the ATA.

Amy Johnson may have assumed she would be chosen to command the ATA's women. Although the Director of Civil Aviation, Sir Francis Shelmerdine, had been the best man at Johnson's wedding, a memo written by him noted that Gower (unlike Johnson) 'had never been a stunt pilot with all the publicity which is attached to that role.' Johnson herself noted that, had she played her 'cards right and cultivated the right people', she may have been given the job. Although Gower quickly sent her a letter asking her to join the ATA, Johnson refused. By 1940, she was desperate for work but still she hesitated to join the ATA. Only days before Germany invaded France, she agreed to take the standard ATA flying test. Yet on arrival, Johnson wrote, 'I suddenly realised I could not go in and sit in line with these girls (who all more or less look up to me as God!), so I turned tail and ran.'

As Britain's situation began to worsen, Johnson decided she could not procrastinate any longer and she joined the ATA 'for the time being'. In the first weeks of her service with the ATA she wrote, 'I dislike intensely being with the ATA...I'm too much of an individualist to work as a cog in a wheel', but later revised her opinion and in a letter described Gower as 'grand'. She was recognised wherever she went and 'RAF pilots... crowded round her plane to ask this seasoned flyer about her solo trip to Australia and her other record-breaking journeys.'

On 3 January 1941, Johnson delivered an aircraft to Prestwick, from where she picked up another aircraft, an Airspeed Oxford, for delivery to Kidlington the following day. She decided to break the journey by landing at Squire's Gate and stay with her sister Molly in Blackpool for the night. There, she confided that the aircraft's compass appeared to be faulty but she dismissed a suggestion that it be checked, telling her sister that she would 'smell her way' to Kidlington. The weather the following day was very poor and more than one person advised her against flying but Johnson responded by saying she would 'go over the top' of the heavy clouds and fly in clear skies.

At 11.49am, Johnson took off and almost certainly

South African ATA pilot Jackie Moggridge. One of the few pilots flying the same day Amy Johnson died, she wrote vividly of the fear stimulated by the poor weather that day.

became lost on her way to Kidlington. Freezing cloud blanketed the UK, rendering visual identification of landmarks very difficult and causing other pilots flying that day to turn back to their airfields. Although Johnson was an experienced navigator and able to fly 'blind', her compass may have been, as she feared, inaccurate. Dipping below the overcast to verify one's position was fraught with danger, due to barrage balloons and bored anti-aircraft gunners around the UK.

ATA pilots Lettice Curtis, Jenny Broad, Audrey Sale-Barker, Gabrielle Patterson and Pauline Gower. Sale-Barker was a pre-war skier and model; Patterson was the first British woman to earn an instructor's licence.

Despite her skill and courage, Johnson found herself in the situation dreaded by every pilot. After three and a half hours, the Oxford's fuel almost exhausted, she donned her parachute and after throwing out a pair of bags, followed them out of the aircraft. She had the bad luck to bail out

ATA pilots attend a briefing before ferrying their aircraft to RAF units around the UK, in a photograph taken in 1944.

Four women of the ATA stand next to an Airspeed Oxford, c.1943. Some 164 women served with the ATA during the Second World War.

over the Thames Estuary. It was now mid-afternoon and it was snowing gently as the light began to fade: the water was almost freezing. The crew of HMS *Hazlemere*, escorting a convoy in the estuary, saw Johnson's parachute drop gently into the water. *Hazlemere* was soon near her and she could be heard calling 'Hurry, please hurry' (the same words she had used years earlier after the *Seafarer*'s crash in the USA), but she failed to catch the lines thrown to her and slipped out of reach of a crewman who leaned out to her from the ship. At this point, *Hazlemere* ran aground and her engines were put into reverse. The ship's captain, Lieutenant-Commander Walter Fletcher, jumped to her rescue but, as he did so, a wave lifted the *Hazlemere*'s stern and Johnson disappeared under the ship's spinning propellers. Johnson's luggage, which Fletcher probably mistook for another survivor, was later recovered. The brave captain spent twenty minutes in the bitterly cold water and later died of exposure and shock. Amy Johnson's remains were never found.

Although other ATAs would die in later flying accidents, the accident rate of ATA women was lower than that of their male colleagues, a statistic which provided one of the best answers to their doubters. Although the notion of women serving remained controversial in some quarters, Pauline Gower proved an excellent choice as their primary advocate. She worked for her women to receive pay equal to that of their male colleagues, a considerable achievement in the 1940s. Her gentle pressure meant that in 1941 the ATA's women began to fly the Hawker Hurricane and the Supermarine Spitfire a few months later. In 1943, Lettice Curtis became the first of eleven women to fly the RAF's large four-engined aircraft. These women formed an elite within an elite – at least in the eyes of their male colleagues. Another of those qualified to fly four-engined aircraft, Rosemary Rees, recalled with exasperation:

The massive size of the Short Stirling bomber is shown in this view with its pilot, the diminutive Joan Hughes.

Having quite an argument with a Wing Commander about a York [a transport descendant of the Avro Lancaster] I was collecting. He said it was so heavy compared with my five foot three and seven stone weight. I pointed out that I was not proposing to attempt to carry it after all, but on the contrary to make it carry me.

There were unexpected dangers to flying. Diana Barnato Walker recalled an incident when flying a powerful Hawker Typhoon:

At about 2,000 feet there was a sudden almighty bang…I glanced down, horrified to see the ground between my legs and feet! No floor! There were the Typhoon's control wires and plumbing, but nothing else. The whole underside of the fighter had blown off in mid-flight…

Reaching Kemble…I decided that, come what may, the undercarriage was going to have to be lowered. I didn't fancy a belly landing with no protection at all underneath…I thought it might hurt…[and] I suddenly realised that I was very, very cold…my teeth started to chatter – not only from the temperature…

[Landing without flaps] I used all the runway [and] taxied up to dispersal where we delivered our aircraft, hoping to be pulled together by the usual cup of strong tea that was always brewing. The duty airman looked out of his shed with a startled expression on his face. 'What on earth happened, Miss Barnato? Why are you bringing us only half an aeroplane?' he gasped…

'I can't help it,' I answered, 'I didn't break it…it just fell apart in the air.'

Pauline Gower did not live to old age. She married in 1945, only to die of a heart attack in 1947 after giving birth to twin boys. Nevertheless, the women of the ATA flew aircraft from the lightest trainer to the heaviest bomber, landed at myriad

A female ATA pilot with a Hawker Typhoon. It was in a Typhoon that Diana Barnato Walker had her terrifying experience, which she recounted phlegmatically in her book, *Spreading My Wings*.

Jackie Cochran's female pilots arrive in the UK. Gower and Cochran stand fourth and fifth from left. A personality clash meant that relations between the two were not always as cordial as publicity suggested.

unfamiliar airfields and coped without radio in all weathers; they showed, beyond doubt, that women could fly as well as men. As a whole, the ATA delivered 308,567 aircraft between 1939 and its disbandment in 1945.

The American version of the ATA's women's section was not as successful. United States Army Air Force (USAAF) General 'Hap' Arnold was approached by the famous (but somewhat egotistical) Jackie Cochran with the idea for a women's organisation within the USAAF; shortly afterwards, in a gesture of Anglo-American goodwill, Cochran was dispatched to the UK with twenty-five of her women pilots, to gain experience and report on the organisation of the ATA. Returning in September 1942, Cochran was infuriated to discover that another pilot

Nancy Harkness Love was a rival to Jackie Cochran both in the air and on the ground. In 1943, the ferrying and training organisations commanded by Love and Cochran were merged.

and rival, Nancy Harkness Love, had been made head of the new Women's Auxiliary Ferrying Squadron. Cochran lobbied for another establishment intended to train women pilots, the Women's Flying Training Detachment, which was duly set up under her command. In August 1943, the USAAF merged the two organisations as the Women's Airforce Service Pilots (WASP), under Cochran's control.

Yet, at this moment, the USAAF began to consider winding the WASP down, partly due to lower-than-expected casualties in Europe. Cochran pressed for 'militarisation' of the WASP (giving them equal rights and status to USAAF officers) but this was rejected in the summer of 1944. In August, Cochran wrote a long memorandum to the USAAF, again pressing for the militarisation of her command. With the future of the WASP in doubt by this stage of the war, Cochran's approach was seen by many as an ultimatum and the WASP was disbanded in December 1944.

This decision was unfair to the women of the WASP, who had endured difficult circumstances to fly 12,650 sorties and deliver aircraft of all types (including the giant B-29 Superfortress) across the USA. The political turmoil caused by Cochran probably did the prospects of women pilots more harm than good for many years after 1945. The unhappy experience during 1944 perhaps prejudiced the WASP in the collective memory and the prospects for women to serve as pilots in the US military. Indeed, the extent of their obscurity was such that the press hailed the 1976 decision by the USAF to admit women to flight training as a first.

Cochran poses with a P-51 Mustang. The unequivocal message says it all: Cochran is said to have wanted a female 'air force', with herself in command.

ACCEPTANCE GAINED

IN 1963, DIANA Barnato Walker flew a BAC Lightning to Mach 1.65: 1,262mph, over the North Sea. She was the first British woman to break the sound barrier and for a time became the fastest woman in the world, beating the supersonic records of both Jackie Cochran and her French rival, Jacqueline Auriol. Barnato Walker wrote:

> We passed through the sound barrier…then suddenly, all was quiet…all our sound was left behind us…Ken [Goodwin, sitting beside Walker] suddenly nudged me and said, 'We'll be in Norway soon!'…Oh, what an easy aircraft: light, power-controlled and so manoeuvrable…

It so happened that Diana Barnato Walker was diagnosed with cancer in the same week that she broke the sound barrier. With typical courage, she recovered, and lived on until 2008.

The spirit of the early pioneering years did not quite end with the Second World War. Jackie Cochran set numerous records (she became the first woman to exceed the speed of sound in 1953, before achieving 1,429mph in an F-104 Starfighter in 1964) as did her French rival, Jacqueline Auriol (a test pilot who traded the women's speed record with Cochran during the 1950s and early 1960s). Others, however, without the vast experience and political influence of Walker, Cochran and Auriol, sought adventure in the style of the pre-war aviators.

OPPOSITE
Jacqueline Auriol, who vied with Jackie Cochran to be the world's fastest woman, climbs from a Mirage III in preparation for a speed record in the early 1960s.

ABOVE LEFT
Diana Barnato
Walker with
the Lightning
in which she
broke the sound
barrier in 1963.

ABOVE RIGHT
In 1964,
Cochran set
speed records
at the controls
of an F-104C
Starfighter. Her
speed over a
25km course was
an astonishing
1,429mph, more
than twice the
speed of sound.

In June 1966, the forty-four-year-old Sheila Scott arrived at Heathrow at the controls of her Piper Comanche, named *Myth Too*, after circumnavigating the world solo in thirty-three days and three minutes. A slew of aviation awards followed, including the Harmon Trophy previously won by Lady Bailey, Amy Johnson, Amelia Earhart and Jackie Cochran. A year later, Scott took Amy Johnson's old London–Cape Town record.

Sheila Scott endured a difficult childhood and, after nursing, acting and modelling, took up flying at Elstree airfield in 1958. Intelligent and attractive, she divorced in 1950 and subsequently led a chaotic and hectic social life. Nor was Scott a natural pilot: she was a heavy smoker, suffered from anxiety and was a nervous student. Yet, after success in air racing, she attracted the attention of the Piper and Cessna aircraft companies and, obsessed with a round-the-world flight, poured all her money into purchasing *Myth Too*.

Although subsequent record-breaking flights were a success (she was awarded the OBE in 1968), Scott suffered crushing misfortune. By 1971, she had debts of £20,000 and her latest aircraft, *Mythere*, was wrecked on the ground by a cyclone the following year. Her later years were dogged by penury and severe depression. By the time of her records, the days of the individualistic pioneers were coming to an end. Sheila Scott, like Donald Campbell (the British World Land and Water Speed Record breaker), sought to continue (or perhaps rekindle) the heroic years of the 1930s. But they became increasingly marginalised during the 1960s. The Cold War, the space race, Vietnam and the 'counter-culture' conspired to relegate them to the back pages in an age when long-distance passenger flights and even space flight were becoming routine.

Ironically perhaps, it was this pace of change which did most for the cause of women in aviation. In 1965, Yvonne Pope Sintes became the first British woman to become an airline pilot and the first British female aircraft captain in 1972. In 1993, Barbara Harmer became the only woman to fly the supersonic Concorde on a scheduled service. The only other woman to fly Concorde was Jacqueline Auriol.

The USAF opened pilot training to women in 1976 and the North American Space Administration (NASA) followed two years later. One of the first to apply was Sally Ride, and,

After a difficult upbringing and early life, Sheila Scott became one of Britain's most famous and successful pilots, breaking many records during the 1960s.

Despite Scott's success, public interest in record-breaking flights was waning by the 1960s. Increasing debt and the wrecking of her aircraft, *Mythere*, in 1972, conspired to end her record-breaking career.

from 8,900 applicants, she was among the thirty-five selected. In 1983, she was part of the team for the seventh Space Shuttle mission and as such became the first American woman to fly beyond the earth's atmosphere. Following the loss of the shuttle *Challenger* in 1986, Ride was appointed to the Presidential Commission investigating the accident. Although she retired from NASA in 1987, she participated in the investigation into the loss of the shuttle *Columbia* in 2003.

Although Joan Hughes flew the RAF's largest wartime bombers, her small frame made her the ideal pilot for the tiny Demoiselle monoplane in the 1965 film *Those Magnificent Men in their Flying Machines.*

Ride was followed by Eileen Collins, who piloted the shuttle *Discovery* in 1995. Collins, whose childhood hero was Amelia Earhart, carried one of Earhart's scarves with her on the mission. Collins later became NASA's first female mission commander aboard *Atlantis* in 1999. She also distinguished herself as the commander of the first 'return to space' flight in 2005, when she captained *Atlantis* during her final mission for NASA.

Despite the success of the ATA, women would not fly for the RAF until 1991, when Julie Gibson was awarded her RAF

Yvonne Pope Sintes became the first woman to fly for a British airline in 1965. Her breakthrough opened the way for hundreds of others to follow in her footsteps.

wings. In 1994, Joanna Salter became the RAF's first fast jet pilot, when she joined 617 Squadron to fly the Tornado GR1; in the late 1990s, she flew in the No-Fly Zones over Iraq. In 2007, Michelle Goodman became the first British woman to be awarded the Distinguished Flying Cross for her bravery in evacuating a wounded British soldier from Basra aboard a Merlin helicopter.

In the twenty-first century, it is not unusual to find an airliner being flown by a woman, or to learn that women are flying fast jets in missions over the Middle East. Although the 'glass ceiling' has yet to be broken completely, the progress made by women in aviation over the last century or so, often in the face of male scepticism, has been remarkable. It is thanks to those such as Amelia Earhart, Amy Johnson and perhaps, most particularly, Pauline Gower's ATA 'girls', that women have cemented their place in aviation history. And, even more importantly, its future.

Sally Ride was chosen from thousands of applicants to join the NASA Space Shuttle programme. She went into space in 1983, becoming the first American woman to fly beyond the earth's atmosphere.

Eileen Collins' childhood hero was Amelia Earhart. As a tribute, Collins carried one of Earhart's scarves with her aboard the shuttle *Discovery* in 1995.

FURTHER READING

Barnato Walker, Diana. *Spreading My Wings*. Patrick
    Stephens, 2003.
Boase, Wendy. *The Sky's the Limit: Women Pioneers in
    Aviation*. Osprey, 1979.
Cadogan, Mary. *Women with Wings: Female Flyers in Fact
    and Fiction*. Macmillan, 1992.
Gillies, Midge. *Amy Johnson: Queen of the Air*. Weidenfeld
    & Nicolson, 2003.
Lovell, Mary S. *Amelia Earhart: The Sound of Wings*.
    Little, Brown, 1989.
Mackersey, Ian. *Jean Batten: The Garbo of the Skies*.
    Macdonald, 1991.
Markham, Beryl. *West with the Night*. Virago, 1984.
Moscrop, Liz and Sanjay Rampal. *The 100 Greatest Women
    in Aviation*. Aerocomm, 2008.
Schroder, Helena Page. *Sisters in Arms: The Women Who Flew
    in World War II*. Pen & Sword, 2006.
Whittell, Giles. *Spitfire Women of World War II*.
    Harper Collins, 2007.

PLACES TO VISIT

Brooklands Museum, Brooklands Road, Weybridge, Surrey
    KT13 0QN. Telephone: 01932 857381 ext.221. Website
    www.brooklandsmuseum.com (birthplace of British aviation,
    where many, including Hilda Hewlett, learned to fly)
Imperial War Museum London, Lambeth Road, London
    SE1 6HZ. Telephone: 020 7416 5000.
    Website: www.iwm.org.uk/visits/iwm-london
Imperial War Museum Duxford, Duxford, Cambridgeshire
    CB22 4QR. Telephone: 01223 835000.
    Website: www.iwm.org.uk/visits/iwm-duxford

Maidenhead Heritage Centre, 18 Park Street, Maidenhead,
   Berkshire SL6 1SL. Telephone: 01628 780555.
   Website: www.maidenheadheritage.org.uk (contains an
   exhibition dedicated to the ATA)
Royal Air Force Museum London, Grahame Park Way,
   London NW9 5LL. Telephone: 020 8205 2266.
   Website: www.rafmuseum.org.uk
Royal Air Force Museum Cosford, Shifnal, Shropshire
   TF11 8UP. Telephone: 01902 376200.
   Website: www.rafmuseum.org.uk/cosford
Science Museum, Exhibition Road, South Kensington,
   London SW7 2DD. Telephone: 0333 241 4000.
   Website: www.sciencemuseum.org.uk (exhibits include
   Amy Johnson's *Jason*)
Sewerby Hall and Gardens, Church Lane, Sewerby,
   Bridlington, East Riding of Yorkshire YO15 1EA.
   Telephone: 01262 673769.
   Website: sewerbyhall.co.uk (houses an important
   collection of Amy Johnson artefacts)

USA

Amelia Earhart Birthplace Museum, 223 North Terrace Street,
   Atchison, KS 66002. Telephone: 001 (913) 367 4217.
   Website: www.ameliaearhartmuseum.org
International Women's Air & Space Museum, Burke
   Lakefront Airport, Rm 165, 1501 N. Marginal Road,
   Cleveland, OH 44114. Telephone: 001 216 623 1111.
   Website: www.iwasm.org
Smithsonian National Air and Space Museum,
   Independence Avenue at 6th Street, SW, Washington,
   DC 20560. Telephone: 001 202 633 2214.
   Website: www.airandspace.si.edu (houses Amelia
   Earhart's Lockheed Vega)

INDEX